EARLY MAN

BOOKS BY THE SAME AUTHOR

Egypt, The Black Land
The Face of the Past
Riddles of the Sphinx

SUTTON POCKET HISTORIES

EARLY MAN

PAUL JORDAN

SUTTON PUBLISHING

First published in the United Kingdom in 1999 by
Sutton Publishing Limited · Phoenix Mill
Thrupp · Stroud · Gloucestershire · GL5 2BU

British Library Cataloguing in Publication Data
A catalogue record for this book is available from the British
Library.

ISBN 0-7509-2221-4

Cover photograph reproduced courtesy of the Neanderthal
Museum, Mettmann, Germany.

 TM ALAN SUTTON™ and SUTTON™ are the
trade marks of Sutton Publishing Limited

Typeset in 11/16 pt Baskerville.
Typesetting and origination by
Sutton Publishing Limited.
Printed in Great Britain by
The Guernsey Press Company Limited,
Guernsey, Channel Islands.

For Sally

Contents

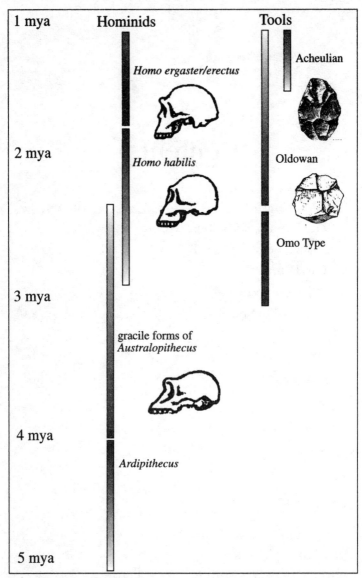

1 mya	Hominids	Tools	
			Acheulian
	Homo ergaster/erectus		
2 mya	*Homo habilis*		Oldowan
			Omo Type
3 mya			
	gracile forms of *Australopithecus*		
4 mya	*Ardipithecus*		
5 mya			

The time charts, here and on p. 44, are intended to help the reader to a quick orientation with dates, human types and tool traditions. They cannot do justice to the complexity of differing situations in different parts of the world over immense time spans.

ONE

The Evolutionary Background

Somehow, during a time-span that stretches between about 7 million and 40,000 years ago, modern humanity evolved out of now extinct forms of apes that were our common ancestors with the chimpanzees and gorillas. After going our separate ways for some 7 million years, we and the great apes of Africa still have about 98 per cent of our genetic material in common. From some tree-dwelling creature with an ape-size brain, who lacked tools, speech, fire and any signs at all of symbolic thought (as the apes still lack all these things in nature except for some rudimentary tool use among the chimpanzees), our ancestral line was transformed into a very big-brained, toolmaking, fire-wielding species that by about 40,000 years ago was beginning to manifest even the most sophisticated traits of modern human behaviour. The paintings of the cave artists of the last ice age are as good as anything that humanity has ever achieved in this line.

Human evolution has taken place against a backdrop of climatic change, which has played a big part – many different parts – in the forging of humanity. The past 7 million years or so have been relatively cold compared with prevailing conditions throughout the long history of the Earth, though there have been warmer fluctuations within the cold (and we are living in one now). There were great ice ages in the very remote past, but the world enjoyed stable warmth again – with little difference in conditions between the poles and the equator – until about 55 mya (million years ago). After that, a slow drop in temperature reached a low (but still not as low as today) between about 35 and 25 mya. These were the times (immensely long times by our standards) when geology and the fossil record tell us that the earliest of the Primates, the order of mammals to which we belong, were evolving and first diversifying.

The very earliest primates (or proto-primates) we can spot in the fossil record were mouse-sized creatures that lived on insects, or slightly larger animals that probably ate leaves and fruit. By about 55 mya, the first primates that resembled something we would recognize today, like tarsiers and lemurs, were flourishing in North America – *Notharctus* is the scientific name given to perhaps the best known of them. These were the first of the primate line to exhibit the noteworthy primate trait of having bigger brains in relation to their body size than is generally the case in the animal world. Big brains in relation to body size indicate cleverness in some direction. With the early primates, the cleverness was probably devoted (in association with colour vision) to spotting and securing high quality food, in the shape of ripe fruits and fresh leaves, against the noisy visual background of a clutter of branches and foliage, especially at night – for the early primates were nocturnal creatures. High quality food could sustain the busy nervous activity of their clever brains without entailing the sort of large and elaborate gut required to extract nourishment from

3

poorer food. In this fashion, a very promising evolutionary feedback process was initiated, involving good food, braininess and gut reduction; it has featured importantly in human evolution.

A further premium that evolution by natural selection put upon primate cleverness arose out of the very social character of most primate lifestyles. Primate 'society' does show considerable variety but most monkeys and apes live in social groups. Now, among animals of every sort, and not just primates or mammals in general, the socially living species are almost invariably the cleverer species. Society brings benefits in the form of mutual support, cooperation and shared defence against the species' enemies, but it also brings liabilities in the shape of quarrels (for example over status, sex and food), damaging competition and greater risk of the spread of disease. So social relationships are an important part of most primate life, and the demands of social life went on to play as big a part in the evolution of primate cleverness as did stereoscopic vision and agility among the branches: in the end, probably a bigger part. Monkeys and

4

apes in social groups prosper because of their mental capacity for negotiating their way through social interactions, for cooperation and selfishness as it suits, for forming alliances and breaking them as situations demand, for guessing at the intentions of their fellows and disguising their own, for buttering one another up and cheating each other by turns. A great deal of brain power is needed to handle a system of social relations with this sort of sophistication – there must be good memory and some capacity to guess at the future and enter into the 'minds' of others, which means having some sort of consciousness of a 'mind' of one's own, if only a socially dedicated 'mind'. For an unimaginably long stretch of time, well into the period of human evolution, it was most likely the social sort of primate intelligence that burgeoned, without any great advances in general intelligence. Even now, psychological tests have revealed that human beings remain particularly adept at solving puzzles with a social dimension, problems cast in terms of possibilities for cheating or countering cheating from others. Essentially the selfsame puzzles served

5

up without the social colouring take longer to solve and are not solved so often. At the other end of the primate scale from ourselves vervet monkeys, for example, are known to be very adept at social behaviour but often quite unintelligent in the face of, to us, clear dangers in their environment.

The lineage that runs from the early primates to our common ancestor with the great apes includes, at about 35 mya, a monkey-like creature we call *Aegyptopithecus*, from the Faiyum lake deposits of Egypt where many related monkey-like forms flourished down to about 31 mya. Their small eye sockets indicate that these were no longer such nocturnal creatures and their teeth suggest that some of them, at least, were already closer to apes and men than monkeys. They were about the size of modern gibbons but they lacked the very long arms of the tree-swinging apes of today.

By about 23 mya, East Africa was home to many sorts of hominoid primates, the Hominoidea being the superfamily to which the apes (including the gibbons as well as the orang-utans, chimps and gorillas) and human beings belong. In the East

African environment of tropical forests and woodlands there were by now few lower primates and very few monkeys, who were probably thriving in some less forested area like North Africa. The cooling of the world, that brought noticeably colder conditions in northern latitudes, saw increased aridity as its chief effect in tropical and subtropical regions – this association of northerly cooling and southerly drying was to go on being repeated as the world got colder still into the time of human evolution. *Proconsul* is the best known of the early apes of East Africa, showing a definite progression from *Aegyptopithecus* towards the apes of today: among the various *Proconsul* species muzzles were shorter than among the monkeys, brains large both relative to body size and in absolute terms, shoulders and elbows suggesting some development of the suspensory, tree-swinging habits seen in modern apes. While some of the earlier monkey-like creatures had tails, these later hominoids of East Africa probably did not. Some of them have dental features that point towards the living apes and humans (with signs that their diet could include hard nuts and tubers as well as soft fruit) but the long arms of today's apes – and to an extent of our earliest ancestors too – were still not in evidence.

The world's climate grew a bit warmer again after about 25 mya, to peak at about 16 mya, but there were further drops in temperature at about 12, 10 and 7 mya, after which a more severe drop heralded the epoch of fluctuating ice ages, basically cold, in which human evolution has occurred and in which we still live, with permanent ice in Antarctica. The factors leading to climatic deterioration, especially over the last few millions of years, include: changes in the heat output of the Sun, which goes up with sunspots and down with less stormy times in the solar atmosphere; variability in the strength of the Sun's heat at the surface of the Earth caused by blocking from volcanic dust in the Earth's atmosphere; changes in the Earth's reception of solar heat as a result of the overlapping effects of variations in the Earth's orbit round the Sun and the angle (and wobble of that angle) of its axis to the plane of the Solar System. There are cycles in most of these factors that mesh together in interactions too complicated to model with any certainty and vulcanism is an additional random factor, but the geological record of the Earth has preserved detailed evidence of the alternation of ice ages and interglacial periods – in cores from ocean beds and from the polar ice caps, in lake sediments, in deposits of wind-blown debris (called loess) that was blown off the regions close to the glaciers, in sequences of pollen grains and animal bones from geological and archaeological sites (some indicating warm and others cold conditions), and in old raised beaches that record changing levels of the sea (for ice ages lock up precipitation in glaciers, and cold contracts the volume of the world's oceans). When data like these are correlated all over the world and dated by all sorts of methods derived from physics, a very useful chronological framework for the evolution of humanity can be constructed.

After about 16 mya, when things began to cool again in the northern latitudes, the tropical and subtropical world once more grew drier and the increasing aridity of the East African environment started to put selective pressure on its early ape inhabitants. The apes of Africa began their retreat into the shrinking tropical forests where they hang on today, though thanks to Africa's collision through continental drift with Europe and Asia some of their relatives were able to spread out into the woodlands of southern Europe and Asia. They have not survived as part of the European fauna, but they continue to inhabit the Far East. The orang-utans are thought to have differentiated from the general ape ancestry at about 12 mya.

Some relative or descendant of *Proconsul* gave rise to the common ancestry of the pongids (chimps and gorillas) and the hominids (human beings) between about 10 and 7 mya. Remains from the Samburu Hills in Kenya reveal a creature with molar teeth rather like those of gorillas today within this time-span. Genetic studies suggest a date of something like 6-7 mya for the divergence between the chimpanzees and the hominid line. In terms of genetics and even way of life, the chimpanzees (particularly, in some respects, the pygmy chimps called bonobos) are our closest non-human living relatives. So long as we always remember that both they and ourselves have experienced 6 million or more years of separate evolution in very different circumstances, the chimps can shed some light on the likely nature of our own remote ancestors, whose remains have not yet been found back beyond about 5 mya and then only in very fragmentary form.

For all that we share over 98 per cent of our genetic material, the differences between chimpanzees and human beings, both in appearance and behaviour, are very great. (The genetic differences, particularly in the area of control gene functions, result in a very different process of development in each human being from that of each chimpanzee; at the same time, we can perhaps recognize, given the genetics in common, that natural selection had not so very much work to do to get from something like a chimp to something like a human being.) Humans, unlike all other primates, can walk bipedally, on their two legs, whereas chimps can at best only walk for short distances in a very awkward fashion on their legs alone: they usually go about on all fours, knuckle-walking with their long arms. Humans have small canine teeth and flat faces

11

with protruding noses rather than the flat-nosed muzzles of the chimps. Humans are relatively hairless and sweat all over. Humans eat (and share) meat on a much more regular basis than chimps do and, among foraging peoples like the Bushmen of South Africa or our direct ancestors of the last ice age, they hunt cooperatively to acquire their meat, which chimps do not do on anything like the same scale. Even human groups still living a 'Stone Age' way of life in remote corners of the world make complicated tools and communicate with complex languages: chimpanzees use rudimentary tools (and can even be said to make tools if we consider stripping side twigs off a stick to be toolmaking) but they speak no language at all. They lack the physiology to produce the sounds needed for speech and it is debatable whether even the most dogged attempts to teach them human sign language have ever got them much beyond the level of grammar represented by 'gimme banana'. No chimpanzee that has picked up a bit of sign language has ever passed it on to its offspring. There have been reports of apes warming themselves in the heat of natural fires, but chimpanzees can neither make fire nor control it when it occurs in nature. Human beings are relatively and absolutely very big-brained by comparison with chimps (and their brains show the asymmetry associated with handedness, which is not so marked in any other creature). Human children are born big-brained and go on to become more so during a lengthy process of postnatal development, during which learning about life proceeds on a scale unknown to chimpanzee infants.

Even so, there are elements of chimpanzee life that do show some faint resemblances to the life of modern, or recently vanished, foraging peoples. Chimps do eat meat occasionally (young monkeys, for example) and sometimes acquire it by means of cooperative hunting operations in a way that no other primates do, except ourselves. But plant food is the main item of their diet and they get it individually and eat it on the spot. They use no weapons in the hunt and no tools to cut up their meat. What tools they use are sticks to poke out grubs and, occasionally, stones to help break up food. They might hang on to stones that have

13

proved their worth but they never fashion them into better tools by knocking bits off them.

Chimpanzee society is based on the females' relationship with their infants. Females tend to forage for themselves, taking plant food and insects. Males roam between the females of their group, on the look-out for sexual opportunities as they arise and warding off rivals as far as they can. On the whole it is the males who undertake the hunting of animal prey, though females do sometimes join in that activity, with some meat sharing as a result. All this is in contrast with the social patterns of modern foraging peoples, characterized by cooperative hunting, meat sharing with fellow hunters and with wives and children, marriage, kinship relations, interchanges by marriage and trade with other tribal groups. To say nothing of language use, a taste for personal decoration, artistic production, complex social networks, and magical and religious practices such as no other creatures display.

Nevertheless, it is in the area of social relations and social strategies within their groups that chimpanzees reveal their most human-like traits of behaviour – even if they are traits that we do not conventionally like to regard as our finest attributes. Chimpanzees have brought the social skills of the primates to heights only exceeded by humanity itself – they manipulate and deceive one another and are very alert to the possibilities of being deceived. It is as though the rest of their life – their food gathering and tool-using, their sexual activity as such and (in the case of the females) their parental concerns – is all very largely conducted on automatic pilot, with 'imagination' and inventiveness only brought to bear on their social relations. To get advantage for oneself in the social context calls for a certain self-consciousness about one's own desires and possibilities, together with an imaginative insight into the probable wants and talents of one's fellows. Imagination and consciousness (and the bigger brains to operate them) look like the products of evolution by natural selection in circumstances favouring their development among competing apes in a particular ecological adaptation. What the 'consciousness' of a chimpanzee feels like is, of course, impossible to say – but then the same might be said about the consciousness of other human beings, even those close to us, and even about our own individual consciousness as it changes from moment to moment and over the course of our lives. For now we may note the baffling unfamiliarity, to us, of the possibility of a form of consciousness almost entirely concerned with social interactions – to the exclusion of the mechanics of food procurement, tool use, the sex act, maternity, etc, etc. For this sort of consciousness, or at least imaginative intelligence, is likely to have been the one that first evolved in our primate ancestry: and probably persisted throughout most of human evolution, too.

Human evolution, like the evolution of the entire living world, has occurred by means of genetic mutation and natural selection. Random changes in the replication from generation to generation of the genetic code that determines each organism's developmental process result now and then in superior adaptive traits. Even a small advantage in life is likely to confer longer survival and a better chance of reproduction to the living thing that possesses it, so that the type persists while less adaptive types drop away. Working blindly and relentlessly through the generations, natural selection produces new forms that can prosper in the multitude of different ecological niches in the world. The big brains and conscious intelligence of modern humanity (and many more traits) have been generated in this way, through the twists and turns of the very changeable world of the last few millions of years. It is at times when small and perhaps rather isolated populations of living things face great environmental change that evolution proceeds at its fastest.

Our common ancestors with the chimpanzees of about 7 mya were not, of course, themselves chimpanzees, though they must have resembled them more than us: a sort of unspecialized chimp, quadrupedal but without the very long arms and knuckle-walking that the chimps (and gorillas) went on to evolve. They were still arboreal in habit, but not too evolved in the direction of the living apes to be unable to scuttle on two legs occasionally over more open ground: an already big-brained (for body size), probably black-coated, fruit and insect eating (and maybe tool-using) forest species that soon split into the chimp and human lines.

The earliest hints in the fossil record of what could be a genuine hominid presence date to between 5 and 6 mya, and new discoveries are regularly made. The Awash Valley in Ethiopia has turned up a very early find, at about 5 mya, that looks ancestral to later East African hominids. From Lothagam in Kenya comes a mandible (lower jaw) fragment that may very well stand close (at getting on for 5.5 mya) to the time of separation of the human line from the chimps' ancestry. About a million years later than the Lothagam jaw, a hominid species attested by the remains of several individuals has been found in Ethiopia, with teeth, jaw fragments, some arm parts and a piece of a skull. This latter fragment is particularly important because it preserves the hole in the base through which nerves pass into the spinal column on which the skull sits. In chimps, this hole is not positioned under the skull but rather towards the back because, moving about on all fours, chimps do not carry their heads balanced on their spines but thrust forward, needing strong musculature from the top and back of the skull to keep their heads from hanging on their chests. The hole in the skull fragment of the creature called *Ardipithecus ramidus* from Ethiopia is rather well forward under the weight of the skull, in a way that suggests that evolution towards bipedal walking was already under way. At about 4.4 mya, *Ardipithecus* still shows jaw and teeth details that are mostly very ape-like, though the canine teeth are more hominid in form. All in all, in *Ardipithecus* we can tentatively discern just such first steps towards hominid status as we may expect from a creature still not so far removed (a couple of million years or so) from ape ancestry. Floral and faunal evidence associated with the *Ardipithecus* remains indicate an environment more wooded than was to come later on in East Africa as the drying related to the cooling climate of the ice ages progressed.

Better known than *Ardipithecus* is the hominid genus first named in South Africa in the 1920s, *Australopithecus* (literally 'Southern Ape'). But *Australopithecus* was no ape as we know apes and he was not confined to South Africa. In fact, it is an early Australopithecine species called *Australopithecus anamensis*, who from Kenya at about 4 mya, takes human evolution across the line that definitely separates our ape ancestry from our own lineage. Remains of nine individuals include jaw and leg bones and, while the dental arcade (the U-shaped run of the teeth from molars at the back through front teeth and back to the molars on the other side) shows a still ape-like squareness, the leg bones display clear evidence of bipedal walking. The teeth suggest a mostly vegetarian mode of subsistence and environmental indications are of woodland but with some bush. After this time, climatic changes, perhaps reinforced by mountain building in Kenya and Ethiopia, began to impose an even drier and less wooded world upon our remote ancestors in East Africa. Grasslands spread at the expense of wooded areas and the fossil record demonstrates several instances of faunal evolution in adaptation to the changing conditions. Elephants and rhinos, for example, developed teeth better suited to grazing and chewing than before. The early hominids, too, were an adaptation to grassland life.

Some time after about 4 mya, *Australopithecus anamensis* appears to have given way to a new species we call *Australopithecus afarensis*, whose most famous representative is known to the world as 'Lucy'. This species is represented by the remains of enough individuals, with some fairly complete specimens like 'Lucy', to make a fuller account of the physical characteristics and way of life of *Australopithecus afarensis* than we could with any earlier hominid finds from East Africa. At Hadar in Ethiopia the remains were found of at least thirteen individuals who had evidently all met their end together, perhaps in a flash flood. Males were evidently much taller than females, at about 1.5 m against 1 m, and very much heavier at an estimated 65 kg vs. 30 kg. This sort of sexual dimorphism makes *A. afarensis* look more like the harem-keeping gorillas of today than the more sexually flexible chimpanzees: it may have more to do with a protective and defensive male role in the hazardous open grasslands than with male rivalry. Brain size, at between 350 and 500 ml, was in the ape range but big for body size, in skulls with projecting muzzles and sloping foreheads.

Canine teeth were smaller than those of apes and the molars were now bigger, as though designed for chewing harder stuff off the grasslands, like nuts and seeds. However, the short legs and long arms of 'Lucy' and her kind point to a way of life that was still partly arboreal – perhaps sleep was still sought in the protective cover of remaining woodland patches. But the short and broad blades of the pelvis and details of the bones of thighs, knees and feet are indicative of a bipedal walking gait. All in all, there can be no doubt that these early hominids of East Africa were lately descended from some common ancestor of the humans and apes. The evolving apes faced a slow decline in the shrinking forests of ice age times: the evolving humans were to go on to great things in the end.

TWO

From Apeman to Early Man

Various sorts of *Australopithecus* were probably quite widespread in the less wooded parts of Africa after some 4 mya, not just in East Africa. A find has been reported from Chad and the discovery of a very early form of Australopithecine has been announced in South Africa. At between 3.6 and 3.2 mya, this find represents the most skeletally complete specimen of *Australopithecus* discovered to date. Foot bones confirm its bipedal status, though some features have been interpreted as indicating a certain extent of tree-living too, and it may be that South Africa was not at this time as unwooded as East Africa. A slightly later species called *Australopithecus africanus* is already well-known from South Africa and seems in some ways to show an evolutionary advance (in the direction of humanity at least) over East Africa's

A. afarensis, with smaller canines, bigger molars, a slightly flatter face, a higher forehead and less of the sexual dimorphism of the East African forms. But the relationships of all the various sorts of Australopithecines make a tangled web on which the last word in the way of classification remains to be said. (There is a broad division between slender forms like *afarensis* and *africanus* and a more robust range that evolved a little later (about 2.5 mya), but lines of descent in different parts of Africa are not yet altogether clear. The robust types, with their huge jaws and heavy skull architecture, look like a very specialized adaptation to chewing hard vegetable matter and it is unlikely that any of them played a part in evolution towards humanity.)

It seems probable that the slender types, called graciles by the anthropologists, would have been at least as handy in the tool-using and toolmaking line as are the chimpanzees today. Bipedal posture, freeing the hands from locomotion (except for sojourns in the trees), is likely to have facilitated tool use over and above that of the chimps, but no stone tools that we can identify have ever been found in association with the gracile Australopithecines. If they were using tools, then those tools were probably made of perishable materials or unmodified stones, like the twigs and hammers of the chimpanzees of today. In that case, the very earliest manifestations of tool use and toolmaking among the hominids will never be recognized by archaeology.

Be that as it may, it is certain that the bipedalism of the early hominids constituted a great step forward in the evolution of humanity. There have been many suggestions to explain the adaptive value of bipedal locomotion and posture. When any thick pelts that our ape ancestors had retained were shed to promote heat loss in the shadeless savanna, then upright bipedalism would have reduced the amount of skin area presented to the heating and damaging direct rays of the sun. Bipedalism also gets the head up, away from heat-radiating ground level and into cooler breezes. It made it possible to peer over the grasses of the savanna for early warnings of enemies and prey, to run down or run away from. It may even be that bipedalism evolved in the first instance not to maintain life in the savanna but to traverse it as

quickly as possible and get back into the shelter of
the shrinking woodland patches of the aridifying
world of the times. All these explanations plausibly
relate bipedalism to the ecological changes that saw
woodland continually giving way to grassland during
the several millions of years of early hominid
evolution. There was an adaptive niche for a
specialized ape (almost, we might say, an ex-ape)
that could start to exploit the new environment.

With bipedal adaptation to grassland living, there
came not just survival in a changing world but fresh
opportunities. Standing up and walking freed the
hands to carry stones and throw them when danger
or a chance to kill some small animal arose. The
hands were also free to evolve into better agents of
manipulation in concert with improving mental
performance by better brains. Those brains now
found a novel world to look into with their long-
evolved primate acuity of vision: a world of great
depth in distance with varied details dotted around
it at different depths, from the small rodent under
foot to the lion troop under distant trees. It has
been suggested that our typical love of landscape

views is owed to this phase of our evolution, when our gaze into such scenes was a source of vital interest. And, of course, there was an evolutionary premium on the better-brained among the Australopithecines who could make best sense of what they saw in the wide world – either to escape the dangers or exploit the opportunities.

Bipedalism must also have altered the visual appearance to each other of the evolving hominids, particularly perhaps where sexual relations were concerned. The big penises and full breasts of the human line may have evolved in step with bipedalism, changing the nature of sexual attractions and helping in the very long run to promote more personalized bonds between food-sharing males and females with their children – with less of the indiscriminate mating seen among most other primates (including the chimps) who can never keep track of paternity and develop family units in the way that all human societies do. Affording more in the way of full frontal encounters of every sort, bipedalism must in general have enhanced the subtlety of all social encounters, encouraging even more mental agility to negotiate

27

the social scene and perhaps in that way extending the range of facial and vocal signals that underlie the development of language. At all events, bipedalism marks the turning point at which hominids and pongids decisively parted company.

We are lucky to be able to see to this day the most direct realization of the Australopithecines' bipedal status, for some of their actual footprints have been discovered at a place called Laetoli in East Africa (where *Australopithecus afarensis* remains have also been found). These footprints date to 3.6 mya, when the tracks of many animals and even the marks of raindrops were preserved in volcanic ash that hardened in the sun after getting wet in the rain and was subsequently buried under another protective ash fall. Seventy or so hominid footprints run for 27 m and it looks as though they record the stroll of a larger and smaller individual (perhaps male and female or mother and child), side by side, with a third walking in the steps of the larger of the two. Halfway along, they seem to have stopped for a moment to look to the west. The footprint impressions show that their big toes were in line with the rest, like our own, and not opposable like an ape's, and they brought their feet down with a positive strike as we might expect of practised walkers.

It was from the gracile sort of Australopithecines that the genus *Homo* was to arise. We are, all of us in the world today, the sole surviving species of that human genus: *Homo sapiens sapiens*. The first of the human line is represented, at well before 2 mya, by the fossil remains of *Homo habilis*, a species that shows a considerable range of types and may, with further discoveries, be separated into two or more different species in future. Some *H. habilis* specimens exhibit the rather long arms seen in *Australopithecus afarensis*, but the brain size of *habilis* starts where the biggest of Australopithecine brains leaves off and ranges from about 650 ml to 750 ml or so. Teeth are more human in form than Australopithecine teeth, faces flatter, skull bones thinner, foreheads higher. The oldest of the fossils that may be assigned to early *Homo* come from Ethiopia at about 2.5–2.3 mya. A maxilla (upper jaw) fragment from Hadar shows an arcade of teeth yet further removed from the squareness of ape jaws than those of the Australopithicenes. Very significantly, the geological levels of the Hadar find – at some 2.3 mya – also contain very early stone tools, while another Ethiopian site has yielded tools in association with hominid remains and claimed evidence of butchery on animal bones at a slightly earlier date.

Toolmaking in stone goes back beyond 2.5 mya, however. We recall that no manufactured tools have ever been found with gracile Australopithecine remains, so it seems reasonable to conclude that toolmaking in stone was from the first associated with the evolution of *Homo* out of *Australopithecus* in the form of something like *Homo habilis*. The oldest tools known, rough flakes smashed off pebbles, have been discovered in Ethiopia and are called after the Omo region in which they were found, dating back to about 3 mya. In the dry savanna landscape, it was along the beds of rivers and streams and by ponds and lakes that our earliest ancestors lingered, coming to water alongside other grassland species. In these places small game might be available and pebbles suitable for toolmaking might be found.

By the time of the *Homo* jaw fragments from Hadar, the simple pebble smashing in Omo style had evolved into the first industrial tradition of any real distinction, which we call Oldowan after Olduvai Gorge in East Africa where it was first recognized. The Oldowan, too, was based on pebbles, using as tools both the knapped flakes and the cores that were left after removing the flakes. The flakes could cut and the cores could chop. Finds of broken animal bones in association with these early tools suggest their use on meat-bearing animal parts, whether scavenged from other creatures' kills or hunted by the hominids themselves. Evidently the low level of meat eating seen among today's chimpanzees had already been exceeded by the early hominids, providing them with convenient packages of energy-rich nutrition to keep them going on the savanna, so long as they could catch or scavenge enough of it. Both catching prey and scavenging under threat from carnivorous rivals like the lion or dedicated scavengers like the hyena required mental alertness and cooperative work: nature continued to put a premium on brainpower. (Predatory animals in general tend to be large brained.) Toolmaking to a regular and socially

31

shared pattern also called for good brains capable of a sequence of operations in line with a concept of the finished product, however unconsciously carried out. The Oldowan tools are pretty crude products and it took a million years for them to evolve into anything better, but they mark a great progression in human evolution. Ground living, toolmaking and meat eating are the trinity of adaptations that made early humanity out of former apes.

In some cases, it is possible even at these earliest stages of toolmaking in stone to determine that the implements are the products of mostly right-handed makers. Human beings are the only markedly handed primates and the brain asymmetry associated with handedness appears also to be involved in the capacity for language use. Toolmaking and language use can easily be seen to have features in common – the sequence of steps necessary to make a stone tool according to some regular pattern does resemble the sequence of sentence building with mutually understood words, and tools stand in a similar role between ourselves and the external world to the role filled by language in handling, inside our heads, the world outside ourselves. A finished tool has elements of past, present and future about it in a way that resembles our use of tenses in language: actions carried out on a raw stone in the past have brought about its present condition with a view to using it for some future (if not very future) task.

The asymmetrical brains of *Homo habilis* suggest the incipience of language use, though the parts of the vocal tract that would help us to establish the larynx position of these creatures have not yet been found. Certainly the balancing of the skull on top of the spinal column seen since *Australopithecus* would have initiated the necessary changes in the flexing of the underside of the skull and jaw position that eventually resulted in the capacity to vocalize in a way chimps can never do. The beginnings of language were probably seen among *habilis* groups, as crude in utterance and limited in range of expression as the rough, undeveloped and unvarying stone tools of the time. To judge by the extremely slow progress of toolmaking techniques, we may conclude that language evolution was to be just as protracted, remaining for millions of years at a level little better than a sort of vocalized version of the mutual grooming habits of the apes. Language may have been pregnant with possibilities for ultimate expansion into abstract thought, but its long initial manifestation is likely to have been very limited in scope and largely employed in the social sphere, in line with the special character of primate cleverness. Basic language competence, even today, does not appear to rely on very much in the way of brain circuitry.

The daily life of *Homo habilis* was a very simple affair, with no unambiguous evidence of home bases having any sort of built structures or use of fire. Much food probably still came in the form of vegetable matter, but the animal bones (of pig, antelope, horse, even elephant, hippo, rhino and some carnivores) found in association with Oldowan tools sometimes carry cut marks establishing that the tools were used to process the meat on those bones. They also often carry the teeth marks of carnivores, indicating that at some stage, either before or after early *Homo* went to work on them, they were subject to the attentions of predatory animals. Whether early *Homo* scavenged or hunted, or both, is not easy to say for certain. But, even if early man was mostly a scavenger, he was certainly a top scavenger of the food chain, making his mark on the natural world of which he was a part. Possibly the distinctively human trait of meat sharing with fellow hunters and with females and children back at base had its first beginnings with *Homo habilis*. In the aridifying world of the early hominids, food sharing would have been an adaptively useful trait. In that case, the prototypes of family life, with males provisioning and caring for their females and children in more or less monogamous relationships, and of kinship relations, may have begun their evolution at about this time.

The remains assigned to *Homo habilis* exhibit a great range of variability, with marked size differences that may be attributable to more than sexual dimorphism. Some specimens show features that foreshadow the physical characteristics of the next stage of human evolution, with very marked brow-ridges and a more angular shape to the back of the skull, while the facial area can be rather more tucked in under the vault of the brain case, with a more prominent nose. The postcranial skeletons of various sorts of *Homo habilis* can also vary considerably, some individuals still displaying the short-legged, long-armed pattern that goes back to the Australopithecines and others looking longer-legged like subsequent humanity.

Homo habilis fades from the fossil record at about 1.8 mya; by about this time the next stage of human evolution is in evidence in Africa, and perhaps in other parts of the world too. It can be argued that some of the *habilis* specimens we have, like the individual from Koobi Fora in East Africa known as '1470', were already on their way to that next stage of human evolution, *Homo ergaster* and *Homo erectus*, by about 1.9 mya. Certainly '1470' has a large brain at 775 ml, though not yet up to *ergaster/erectus* capacity, but he was found without the arm bones that might distinguish him conclusively from the long-armed *habilis* types. At about the same time, the Oldowan tool tradition gradually gave way to a new and much more distinctive one that we call Acheulian, after the site at St Acheul in northern France where its products were first identified in the last century. The later Oldowan includes bifacially worked pieces that represent a considerable advance on the usually rather roughly flaked core tools of the earlier phases. These bifacially flaked pieces, worked all over their surfaces, are precursors of the so-called 'hand-axes' of the Acheulian, multipurpose tools that show not only a considerable range of types but also some fine workmanship on occasions. Properly bifacial artefacts begin to appear in the African archaeological record at about 1.5 mya. The development of the standardized, all-purpose hand-axe tool surely points to the related development of enhanced mental powers among the successors of *Homo habilis*; and the more highly patterned nature of hand-axe manufacture, involving more steps in the making and better previsioning of the finished product, is likely to have been mirrored in a more structured and standardized use of language.

Something like the Oldowan tradition has been found out of Africa at apparently very early dates, going back to nearly 2 mya (in Israel, Georgia, even Pakistan and China), and in some parts of the world, like the Far East beyond India, no Acheulian tradition was ever adopted. So it is quite possible that early man in the form of a creature like late *Homo habilis*, with nothing better than the Oldowan style of toolmaking, was spreading out of Africa through the Middle East and on to the Far East before the Acheulian ever evolved in Africa itself. In this plausible scenario it was successors of *Homo habilis* who developed the Acheulian hand-axe tradition in Africa (and then sent it out into Europe and the Middle East) while separated successors of the original *habilis* emigrants largely went their own way in the Far East, with not very much contact between the widely separate groups both in terms of toolmaking habits and genetic interchange. Starting with much the same sort of late *Homo habilis* stock, the two groups saw a parallel evolution into the next stage of humanity, essentially very alike in both areas since the same pressures of natural selection were at work upon fundamentally the same genetic make-up, and no doubt some genes did continue to flow back and forth through all the thinly spread human populations along the way from Africa to China and Java.

The post-*habilis* stage of human evolution as represented by finds in the Far East is known as *Homo erectus* and many anthropologists have been happy to call the African finds of the same stage by the same scientific name, emphasizing all that the finds have in common. Anthropologists who think there are some significant differences between the two sorts of finds call the African and European representatives of this stage of human evolution by the name *Homo ergaster*. There remains the possibility that *Homo ergaster* evolved in Africa at about 2 mya (earlier than any of his fossils we yet have to hand) and turned into the slightly different *Homo erectus* in the Far East after some of his descendants reached China and Java by perhaps as early as 1.8 mya. It is as well to remember that the story of human evolution, particularly in its early reaches, must be put together out of often meagre and fragmentary finds that are not always as well dated as we should like. This is why new finds can make so much difference to the picture, not in some fundamental way that overthrows everything we thought before (as newspapers are apt to report these matters) but certainly in areas of emphasis upon the significance of one piece of evidence over another. With the establishment of *Homo ergaster/erectus*, the fossil record becomes fuller and we encounter a form of humanity altogether more like ourselves than what has gone before.

The oldest *ergaster* finds in Africa date back to about 1.75 mya but they are rather fragmentary at that early date. From 1.6 mya, however, comes the very complete *ergaster* skeleton known as the 'Nariokotome Boy'. This is by far the most complete skeleton of the *ergaster/erectus* stage of human evolution from such an early date. The skull itself is so well preserved that, for the first time in the story of evolving humanity, we can determine the brain size of an individual with exactitude. On the strength of his teeth characteristics, the 'Nariokotome Boy' was evidently about eleven years old but already some 1.6 m tall, with a cranial capacity of about 880 ml. Without the evidence of the teeth, we might judge the boy to have been aged about fifteen years at death, so it is likely that the rate of physical maturation ran faster in those distant days than it does with us – childhood, with its long period of growth and learning, was not as extended as it is nowadays, though it was already longer than with the apes of today. It is estimated that, had he reached full adulthood, the Nariokotome individual would have attained 1.75 m in height and a brain size of about 900 ml. The brain size of modern human beings, at some 12–1500 ml on average, is about three times larger than we would expect for primates of our overall body size, so the Nariokotome *ergaster* type was already well on the way to the modern human ratio of brain to body size. In fact, brain size doubled between about 2.5 mya, with the late Australopithecines, and 1 mya with *ergaster* and *erectus*: from something hardly outside the ape range (though biggish for body size) to a capacity only about one-third less than the brains of people today. This increase can be partly related to an overall increase in body size but is also clearly indicative of growing brainpower in absolute terms. As our brains have grown evolutionarily, there has been some relative loss in areas associated with smell, sight and even motor control (we gave up leaping about in the trees, after all) but there have been big gains in the neocortical parts of the brain, which are considered to handle complex data in a less purely instinctive way and to be associated with language use and conceptual thought. Very interestingly, the larynx area in *ergaster/erectus* fossils, where they retain it, appears to fall midway between the positions seen in the Australopithecines and in modern humans, strengthening the supposition that language use was developing, however slowly, along with physical evolution. Details of nose and ear that have been preserved in some specimens also chart progress away from ape and towards fully human characteristics. The teeth of *ergaster/erectus* are smaller than those of his ancestors, the molars particularly reduced in relation to the incisors and canines. This situation is evidence for more in the way of meat eating, with emphasis on biting and tearing at the front of the mouth rather than chewing (of vegetable matter) at the back. The entire skull architecture of the *ergaster/erectus* phase (and subsequent ones, too, until the arrival of modern humanity) points to the need for hefty and securely anchored musculature to work the front teeth in heavy, chinless jaws: marked brow-ridges, bars of bone at the back of the skulls and sometimes even keels along the top mid-lines of Asian *erectus* skulls, in particular, attest to strong musculature.

The rest of the skeleton below the skull is very similar in the 'Nariokotome Boy' (and in other *ergaster/erectus* skeletal remains too) to that of modern human beings, with a fully bipedal status and limb proportions essentially like our own. Where the 'Nariokotome Boy' differs from modern youths is in details like the longer spines on some of his vertebrae and the slightly constricted aperture of the spinal canal through the vertebrae (which may have some bearing on chest muscle control in using breath for speech). The pelvis is rather narrow and the neck leading to the ball of the femur (thigh bone) is rather elongated. One should be careful not to make too much of what might be the individual peculiarities of one specimen – human beings are a varied lot at the best of times. At any rate, it looks as though, with the *ergaster/erectus* phase of human evolution, the postcranial skeleton had achieved fundamentally its modern form and stature (though we cannot be so sure about the soft parts within the trunk). Henceforth human physical evolution was to be predominantly a matter of changes in skull architecture and in the size and shape of the brain.

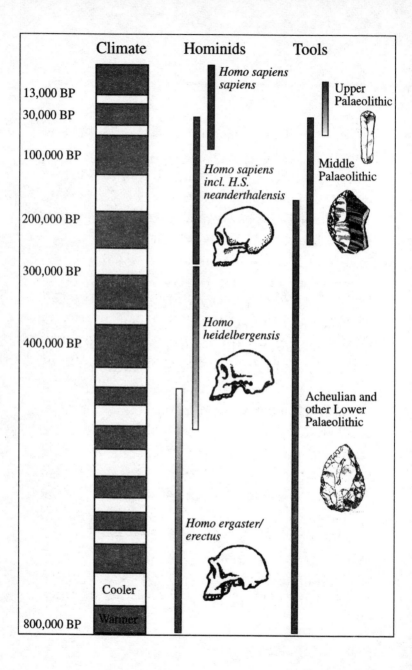

Climate	Hominids	Tools

13,000 BP

30,000 BP

100,000 BP

200,000 BP

300,000 BP

400,000 BP

800,000 BP

Homo sapiens sapiens

Homo sapiens incl. H.S. neanderthalensis

Homo heidelbergensis

Homo ergaster/ erectus

Upper Palaeolithic

Middle Palaeolithic

Acheulian and other Lower Palaeolithic

Cooler

Warmer

THREE

The Human Line

With the *ergaster* and *erectus* species of the genus *Homo*, the ongoing line of human evolution could be said to be well established. What differences there are between African *ergaster* and Asian *erectus* skulls include details like averagely smaller African jaws and molars, with less incidence of keeling along the top of the skulls in keeping with a somewhat reduced call for massive musculature to work the jaws. Some anthropologists see in *ergaster* a clearer foreshadowing of later evolutionary developments in Africa and Europe that would lead on towards modern humanity. In the matter of toolmaking, there is a clear distinction between the habits of the African and European *ergaster* types and the Far Eastern *erectus* populations. The people in Africa and Europe (when they spread there out of Africa by about 1 mya) were often exponents of the Acheulian hand-axe tradition, while the people of the East never adopted the hand-axe and went on with a toolmaking style that, in terms of stone use at least, remained essentially Oldowan. (It is speculated that they may have elaborated the use of perishable but at the time very serviceable materials like bamboo for their toolmaking.) There are some signs, though not always very well dated, that the first spread of toolmaking into Europe was itself of an Oldowan rather than Acheulian character. Oldowan-type tools and a jaw fragment of *ergaster* character are reported at a site in Georgia at 1.8 mya. It may be that, even after the Acheulian was developed in Africa by about 1.4 mya, the fringes of early humanity were still employing the Oldowan sort of tool manufacturing tradition as they spread out of Africa into the Levantine area and around the Mediterranean.

At 'Ubeidiya in the Jordan Valley a basically Oldowan tradition of stone tools shows proto-Acheulian tendencies at between 1.4 and 1.2 mya, as though the Acheulian tradition was diffusing out from Africa after its inception there a few hundreds of thousands of years before. The Jordan Valley is a continuation north of the Great Rift Valley of East Africa and the two regions often enjoyed a similar ecological character in the past, making the Levant an obvious route for African developments to take on their way to the wider world. Sites like le Vallonet and Soleihac in France show an Oldowan sort of toolmaking that may date from about 900,000 BP (years before the present), as may the similar material from Kärlich in Germany, and there are several more sites in Europe with Oldowan-like tools that may go back as far, though they are not always well dated. Fossil human remains to go with these early evidences of toolmaking in Europe are few and far between but we may expect them to belong to an *ergaster/erectus* sort of early human being: the fragmentary discoveries from Gran Dolina in Spain, dating to about 780,000 BP, include some teeth, jaw and skull pieces together with hand and foot bones from four individuals.

The real Acheulian with clear-cut hand-axe production appears to have reached Europe at about 600,000 BP and is found at many sites from Spain in the south to southern England in the north. (Even after the arrival of the Acheulian, Europe still harboured a range of axeless flake tool industries, particularly, though not exclusively, in the east.) Climatic fluctuation was by now the established pattern and, especially in more northerly areas as the world grew cooler overall, it seems inconceivable that the spread of humanity could have been achieved without the use of fire and the occupation of rock shelters and caves. The earliest evidence suggesting human control of fire comes from Africa. At Koobi Fora in East Africa, tools of a late Oldowan type (on their way to Acheulian) have been found in association with deposits of baked earth at a date of about 1.6 mya. The baked earth took the form of a bowl-shaped feature of oxidized soil indicative of higher temperatures than those that result from accidental grassland conflagrations, strongly suggesting human agency. At another East African site, lumps of burnt clay were found in association with stone tools and animal bones at a date of about 1.5 mya; the largest lumps, reportedly found within a hearth-like arrangement of stones, had been heated to a temperature estimated at between 400 and 600°C, again beyond the expected range of naturally occurring fires. At Swartkrans in South Africa, burnt bones of about 1 mya are thought to have undergone temperatures we associate with camp-fires rather than wild fires. We cannot know whether these fires, if they truly were controlled by early human beings, were purposefully lit by some method of fire-making – more likely, natural grassland fires (perhaps as a result of lightning strikes) were kept alight and carefully conserved for long-term use. And whether any 'camps' that went with these very early African 'camp-fires' were worthy of the name of home bases, as some archaeologists have proposed, is similarly unclear. Patterns of large stones with barren zones, where perhaps wind-breaks or protective barriers of thorn bush were piled up, have been identified in the archaeological record, but opinion is divided about the significance of such finds, for natural causes like floodwater or animal activity could account for some of the evidence. But regular use of fire, especially perhaps out of Africa in colder zones where caves were obvious places of shelter, increases the likelihood that home bases of some sort were a feature of the *ergaster/erectus* way of life. The fireside provided not only a source of warmth and defence against foes, but also heat to thaw out and smoke (if not to cook) food, and light to prolong the daytime activities of life (like toolmaking, for example); above all, perhaps, it promoted social life as the scene of mutual grooming (with the growing resource of language use), meat sharing, proto-familial and kinship relations, care and 'education' of the young.

In Europe, hard evidence for the use of fire goes back to perhaps 400,000 BP at a site on the south coast of Brittany; at another near Nice on the Mediterranean, a hearth-like focus with burnt mussel shells has been identified among stones that possibly anchored some sort of shelter of wooden poles and maybe animal skins. There are further sites in France, Germany and Syria that really do suggest the building of structural features to improve on natural places of shelter, in some cases dated back to perhaps 900,000 BP. Fire and built shelter indicate that early man was finding a use for his enlarging brain in an increase of intelligence applied to technical matters, even if it was still social intelligence that probably dominated his dawning consciousness of himself and his kind.

Fire and the occupation of caves allowed human expansion into areas not previously habitable in the cooling times that came on in earnest after about 800,000 BP. Even so the really cold places close to the intermittently expanding ice sheets of the north remained closed to humanity. Early man probably sallied out of Africa and into Europe in the first place via the region of the Levant and around the Mediterranean (though direct crossing from North Africa to Spain may have been feasible at times when glaciation lowered global sea levels). The spread to the Far East probably followed the coastal areas adjacent to the Arabian Sea and the Bay of Bengal, then north into China and south to Sumatra and Java. Java itself was sometimes connected to the Asian mainland during times of low sea level, but there is an island in the Java Sea where *Homo erectus* remains have been discovered that appears never to have been reachable except by a sea crossing – at about 800,000 BP, and presumably by some sort of raft! Growing intelligence in technical matters certainly seems to be attested in this case.

In China, *Homo erectus* remains have been found in contexts dating back to about 1 mya (and, on some evidence, half as much again), but the best known of the Chinese *erectus* finds come from a site near Beijing that is now known as Zhoukoudian. *Homo erectus* from Zhoukoudian was formerly known as 'Peking Man'. The climatic indicators of the site, together with evidence of ancient fluctuations of the Earth's magnetic polarity, suggest a date going back to some 450,000 BP for *erectus* at Zhoukoudian, putting 'Peking Man' into one of the warmer interglacial periods of the ice age era, at a time when the climate of northern China was about the same as it is today. There is evidence for the use of fire on the site and stone tools (in coarse quartz and quartzite) have been found in some abundance there but they are of the simple sort that would be called 'Oldowan' in Africa, where the Acheulian tradition was about 1 million years old by the time. The remains of about forty *erectus* individuals have been found at Zhoukoudian, including fragments damaged in a way that might suggest 'cannibalism' among the occupants of the site. 'Cannibalism' has been proposed to explain the condition of some of the bones from Gran Dolina in Spain, too, at perhaps as far back as 780,000 BP.

When we speak of cannibalism, we are almost always referring nowadays to a ritual activity to do with beliefs about a spirit world – taking over desirable qualities of the dead or subduing their threatening ghosts, for example. For, except in emergencies, cannibalism is not a very worthwhile way of securing food: there is almost always something better to be had in the natural world. So any evidence for cannibalism in the remote past always raises the possibility that we might be faced with the first inklings of ideological beliefs in the evolving human consciousness. Unfortunately, the evidence is rarely very positive and usually open to other interpretations and, in any case, it is very difficult to guess at the states of mind of the people who might have engendered it. Any other signs of ideology from this remote epoch – in the form of possible artistic productions, for example – are noticeable by their almost total absence. The fine finish of some of the African and European hand-axes looks like a glimmering of aesthetic sensibility; there are occasional parallel lines and arcs scratched on bone fragments that do not altogether look like the results of cutting up pieces of meat for food; odd cases of pecked markings on stone or even a stone apparently selected for a faint resemblance to the human form; and occasional finds of pieces of ochre suggest themselves as colouring materials, for skins animal or human? But there is not the slightest sign of representational art or a consistent symbolism of any sort.

By the time of 'Peking Man' and his contemporaries in Java, all solidly *Homo erectus* in character with a brain size ranging between about 900 and 1000 ml, there are strong signs that back in Africa and Europe the human story had already moved on to more evolved forms. (It looks, moreover, as though *Homo erectus* lingered on in the Far East, especially in

Java, for a hundred thousand years or more after the time of the Zhoukoudian finds.) The fragmentary remains from Gran Dolina in Spain may already at some 780,000 BP show signs of evolution out of a late sort of *Homo ergaster* into a species that some anthropologists identify as *Homo heidelbergensis* after a place (actually called Mauer) near Heidelberg in Germany at which an impressive jaw of early man was discovered. The Mauer jaw is a rather massive and chinless affair that would not at first sight look out of place with an *ergaster* or *erectus* skull, but its teeth are small for its build and look forward in some details to the well-known *Homo sapiens neanderthalensis* ('Neanderthal Man') of later times, who was very likely descended from *Homo heidelbergensis* in Europe. The Mauer jaw is not well dated but appears to belong to a warmish period of about 500,000 years ago (just a little earlier than *erectus* at Zhoukoudian). Slightly younger, perhaps, is the rugged shin bone from Boxgrove in England that belongs to some creature of essentially the same *heidelbergensis* character. There are African finds, too, that represent the same post-*ergaster* stage of human evolution, with traits looking forward to modern *Homo sapiens sapiens* himself. A massive skull that convincingly combines *ergaster* features with some of *Homo sapiens* was found in association with Acheulian tools at a place called Bodo in Ethiopia. At an estimated date of 600,000 BP the Bodo skull has the biggest face of all known human fossils, with a very prominent ridge over the eyes and a mid-line keel on the skull top that would be at home on an Asian *erectus* specimen. But the nasal area of the face and the frontal region of the cranium over the brow-ridge are much more modern in form, as are the places on the underside of the skull where the jaw articulated. (Interestingly, there are cut marks on the bone round the eyes, on the cheeks and forehead, at the top and back of the skull that point to defleshing of the Bodo skull at the end of the individual's life, for they never healed: cannibalism again or some other sort of postmortem ritual treatment suggest themselves quite powerfully in this case.) All in all, the Bodo skull is just the sort of cranium we would expect to go with the Mauer jaw and Boxgrove shin, to make up *Homo heidelbergensis.*

The jaw fragment and skullcap from Elandsfontein in South Africa (also known as the Saldanha skull) similarly look like an advance on *ergaster*, with the significantly greater cranial capacity of about 1200 ml: Elandsfontein can conveniently be placed within the same classification of *Homo heidelbergensis* at somewhere between 500 and 200,000 BP to go by associated faunal remains.

Back in Europe, there are finds from the same sort of age range that begin to confirm the evolution of the Neanderthal type out of *heidelbergensis*. The skull from the Caune de l'Arago cave at Tautavel in the French Pyrenees (found along with fragments of some sixty individuals) shows the incipience of Neanderthal traits in its general shape against a background of late *ergaster/erectus* or *heidelbergensis* character. It dates to about 400,000 BP and has a cranial capacity of about 1160 ml, well up on *ergaster* but equally well short of *sapiens*, either Neanderthal or modern. The stone tools found in association with the Arago remains are of the mostly axeless flake type called Tayacian, which is the forerunner of the Mousterian tool kit typically found with 'Neanderthal Man' in later times.

Of perhaps about the same age as the Arago material is the skull from Petralona in Greece: it is certainly older than 200,000 BP and younger than 730,000 BP on geological evidence. The Petralona brain-case comes in at about 1220 ml and, though its shape at the back resembles *ergaster/erectus* skulls, it shows the double brow arch configuration of the later Neanderthalers and their broad nasal opening and inflated cheeks. Not all the classic Neanderthal features are in place, but Petralona fits the bill as European *Homo heidelbergensis* on the way to European *Homo sapiens neanderthalensis*.

In principle, the same transitional stage from *heidelbergensis* to *sapiens* is evident in the skull from the Broken Hill site at Kabwe in Africa, also known by the old name of 'Rhodesia Man'. Here the signs are of a human type on its way from African *Homo heidelbergensis* (as per Bodo) to African early *Homo sapiens sapiens*, with no development of the distinctive traits of *Homo sapiens neanderthalensis* in Europe and western Asia but rather the very beginnings of modern worldwide human features. At first glance, the Kabwe skull looks pretty alien to our modern selves, with its enormous brow arches as its most striking and unmissable feature. But its general shape, with a respectable cranial capacity of about 1300 ml, does look forward to modern humanity, particularly in its steep-sided aspect seen from the back (rather like a tin loaf) and its fullness at the rear when seen from the side. It is at least 125,000 years old and probably older, perhaps to as far back as 300,000 BP. The teeth of the Kabwe skull, incidentally, are unique in the fossil record of early man in showing a degree of dental decay not seen again till the time of the first farmers after about 10,000 years ago. A hole near the left ear may be the result of an attack with some sharp instrument or of the attentions of some fierce carnivore. The arrangement of the voice-box, as inferred from the basal flexing of the Kabwe skull, is thought to suggest a better capacity for forming a wide range of sounds for potential use in speech than is seen in the fossils of earlier forms of humanity – or in the Eurasian Neanderthalers who were evolving at roughly the time of the Kabwe find.

During the time of *Homo ergaster/erectus* and *Homo heidelbergensis*, evolving humanity's postcranial skeleton achieved to all intents and purposes its fully modern form (which, indeed, continues to show considerable variation from person to person and population to population). Brain size increased to the point where it entered the lower part of the range seen in human beings today, poised to increase with the rise of the early *sapiens* species to the averages of modern times (and even exceed them). Those brains were still housed in, to us, outlandish looking skulls disfigured chiefly by the demands of the heavy musculature needed to use the jaws and teeth for purposes that would one day be taken over by better tools and cooking skills. But those brains were also of a different shape from ours and plainly not yet operating in all the clever and inventive ways that ours do. The painfully slow progress of technological innovation (though there was some) and the near total absence of symbolic behaviour attest to this situation.

For all that, early man had come a long way from the Australopithecines in a matter of only a couple of millions of years. It was the ability to exploit an ecological niche (or series of them as the range of human occupation spread into a changing world) under the stern guidance of natural selection that gave the clever ex-apes their chance. Slowly, the resources of the brain were expanding: it was probably still the social domain of the mind that saw the greatest refinements towards self-consciousness as human group sizes grew with more complex relations between individuals, but clearly the technological capacities of the brain were increasing too, with new techniques of toolmaking and shelter building, alongside a growing knowledge of the natural world and how to exploit it to best advantage in the hunt for subsistence in a wide range of environments.

FOUR

The Emergence of *Homo sapiens*

The first really significant improvement in toolmaking practice after the development of the fully bifacially worked hand-axe came at about 250,000 BP in the form of the Levallois technique, named after a Parisian suburb where it was first identified in the archaeological record. The Levallois technique seems to have been developed in East Africa. It represents, for the times, an impressive sophistication of stone tool manufacture, in that it required rather more forethought (consciously or unconsciously applied) as to the intermediate steps needed to achieve the desired end product. The end product of the Levallois technique is a flake of stone whose outer surface has already been so well prepared by preliminary flaking work on the core from which it is to be struck that, once it is knocked off with a final hammer blow, it will require next to no further retouching for use as a projectile point or cutting and scraping tool. The stages of preparatory flaking are conceptually distanced from the climactic strike that delivers the finished tool. We might almost say that the maker of a Levallois point needed to 'see' the finished item in the core of stone he was preparing rather more so than in the case of the maker of an Acheulian hand-axe. Making the axe, you could see the product gradually taking shape in your hands: the Levallois point only jumped out of the mind's eye into tangible presence with the final blow. It is very tempting to think that an improvement in mental performance, afforded by the expansion of the brain after about 500,000 BP towards the lower limits of the modern range of cranial capacity, lay behind the development of the Levallois technique, whose appearance roughly coincides with the first emergence of early *Homo sapiens*. It is also tempting to speculate that the relative sophistication of the technique may have been mirrored in some advancement in the use of language, with perhaps a better sense of tense and logic through intermediate stages of sentence building.

The Levallois technique spread through the Acheulian world, where the production of hand-axes was in any case somewhat in decline in the face of more emphasis on the use of flake tools. But the Levallois style was by no means always adopted for flake tool production thereafter, rather coming and going almost like a fashion – though it was often probably a matter of practicality too, since good stone in liberal quantities is needed to get the best out of the Levalloisian.

The technological traditions represented by the Acheulian and its rather rudimentary flake-based contemporaries are classified by archaeologists as Lower Palaeolithic in Europe or Early Stone Age in Africa. The more sophisticated traditions that came afterwards, with or without Levalloisian technique, are known as the Middle Palaeolithic, or Middle Stone Age in Africa. In Europe and western Asia the Middle Palaeolithic's typical expression is the

Mousterian culture, closely associated with the Neanderthal folk. In the nature of things, stone tools survive in abundance on archaeological sites whereas the bones of their makers are much more rarely found, while items manufactured from perishable organic materials have not often survived either. Middle Palaeolithic people seem to have made little use of bone or antler in their tool production, some of which would have been preserved in the archaeological record if they had had much recourse to it – it is as though their minds were still slow to regard materials from the animal world that they hunted for food in the same light as the stones they employed to make their tools. But some impressive survivals of wooden implements or weapons have come down to us, even from Lower Palaeolithic times. At Clacton in England the pointed tip of a wooden spear dating back to perhaps as long ago as 450,000 BP was found in association with an axeless stone industry. Archaeologists with doubts about the hunting abilities of the people of so long ago have sometimes wondered whether the Clacton spear fragment might have been not a throwing spear but a digging stick or snow probe – both would be interesting enough. But recently several examples of what can only be spears (the largest, at 2.3 m in length, certainly long enough to be a throwing rather than thrusting spear) have been discovered at a site called Schöningen in Germany and dated to about 400,000 BP. The site also yielded up many flint flakes fashioned into points and scrapers and animal bones, mainly of horses, bearing marks of butchery. Another find of a wooden spear in Germany dates to about 125,000 BP.

The human remains found in Europe that continue the story of evolution from *Homo heidelbergensis* towards *Homo sapiens neanderthalensis* are not numerous: populations must always have been small, and deliberate burial in graves seems not to have been a practice until well into Neanderthal times. The Petralona and Arago remains of perhaps about 400,000 BP already displayed some hints of the Neanderthal package of physical features, with a brain size – at about 1200 ml – that was still well below Neanderthal status.

They probably belong to a period at the end of the third most recent ice age or an early stage of the succeeding interglacial period. A little later in that interglacial, skulls from Swanscombe in England and Steinheim in Germany take up the story of European 'neanderthalization'. Swanscombe may be somewhat older than Steinheim, which dates to about 250,000 BP, but essentially the two skulls go well together. The Swanscombe skull bones are thick in a way that harks back to earlier times, but cranial capacity is well up at *c.* 1325 ml; there is a distinctive Neanderthal feature at the back in the shape of a depression called the suprainiac fossa where neck musculature was attached, but the area of the brows is missing where any incipiently Neanderthal brow-ridges would have featured. The female's skull from Steinheim does show brows of the Neanderthal pattern, with separate, rounded arches over each eye: there are also such Neanderthal traits as the suprainiac fossa and taurodont teeth (where large molar pulp cavities reach down into single roots); but the Steinheim woman's skull was rather flat-faced and straight-sided in a fashion more modern

67

than Neanderthal, though she was small-brained at only some 1100 ml.

From the same general time-span as Swanscombe and Steinheim come the remains of at least thirty individuals, including both sexes and children, discovered in a cave system in the Sierra de Atapuerca in Spain. Like Swanscombe, the Atapuerca skull fragments are rather thick and one of the skulls tops the volume of the English skull in reaching about 1390 ml of cranial capacity, though another is in the Steinheim range at 1125 ml. The skulls carried the Neanderthal sort of brow arches and show the mid-face prognathism of the Neanderthalers: their faces look, by our standards, as though they have been pulled forward by the nose. Jaws from the Atapuerca site are massive but show signs of the Neanderthalers' retromolar gap (a space between the last of the molars at the back and the upward part of the jaw that rises to articulate with the underside of the cranium). There are indications from the postcranial bones found in some abundance at this site that the somewhat squat and short-statured body pattern of the later Neanderthalers was evolving here. No tools were found in association with the bones which appear to have been piled up either as a result of human disposal of the dead or, more likely perhaps, of carnivore dumping.

There are further proto-Neanderthal finds from Pontnewydd in Wales – taurodont teeth at about 225,000 BP, and from Biache-Saint-Vaast in France – a long and low skull with the typically Neanderthal bun shape at the back, albeit of small cranial capacity at 1200 ml, dating to between 200 and 160,000 BP. This French skull was found in association with an axeless flake industry of proto-Mousterian character. The beginnings of the Mousterian, so largely identified in its mature form in Europe with the Neanderthal folk, go back in Jersey and in France and Belgium to something beyond 200,000 years ago. All these finds of both human remains and tools date to the time of the last ice age but one – not necessarily to fully glacial times, for there were warmer interstadial episodes within the periods of glaciations.

The bones and tools from Ehringsdorf in Germany may date to such an interstadial of the same penultimate ice age. The tools are, again, of that Tayacian proto-Mousterian sort and the skull pieces come together as more of a Neanderthaler than any of the finds discussed above, though the jaw was still rather massive for a Neanderthal type. The jaw from Montmaurin in France, dated to much the same time or a bit later at about 190,000 BP, is similarly massive but clearly shows the taurodont teeth and retromolar gap of the later Neanderthalers, as does the jaw from the Bourgeois-Delaunay shelter in France which probably dates to the end of the penultimate glaciation at some time before 130,000 BP.

The last interglacial, the warmer period between the penultimate ice age and the latest one that finished about 13,000 years ago, saw the establishment of the Neanderthal type from Western Europe across to western Asia, with an important outpost in the Levantine region at the eastern end of the Mediterranean. The earliest of the clear-cut Neanderthalers may not have been quite as fully Neanderthal as the classic specimens from the last ice age, but many of the typical features were in place. The Neanderthal woman from Saccopastore in Italy was still smaller brained than the later classics but shared the characteristically long and low-vaulted skull when viewed from the side, with suprainiac fossa at the back (but no bun) and projecting face at the front, under developed brow arches. The Saccopastore male was so rugged that his features could be seen as harking back to *heidelbergensis* cases like Petralona. The array of Neanderthalers from Krapina in Croatia, belonging to a late stage of the last interglacial or an early, still not so cold, phase of the last ice age (around 120,000 BP), were even more clearly Neanderthal in character, though a bit more lightly built than the later classics. And the Neanderthal woman whose skull was found in the Tabun cave in northern Israel, in levels dated to about 110,000 BP, was another still small-brained (about 1200 ml) and somewhat gracile but clearly Neanderthal person, with the unmistakable brow-ridge development of the type.

The classic European, western Asian and Levantine Neanderthalers of the last ice age are known in the fossil record by many more remains (however fragmentary on occasions) than any older sorts of early man. They are usually classified, despite their obvious differences from modern and other late fossil humans, as *Homo sapiens* like ourselves, of the subspecies *neanderthalensis* rather than *Homo sapiens sapiens*. The classification is based upon their overall skeletal kinship with the rest of *Homo sapiens* and their large cranial capacities, whose range exceeds the average of today (though their brains were differently shaped in a way that is almost certainly significant). Much of the Neanderthal physique can be interpreted as a thoroughgoing adaptation to the cold of the last ice age. Their compact body shape, with big chests and short extremities, looks like a strategy to conserve internal heat, much as the modern Eskimo build does. Their large noses have been seen as mechanisms to heat cold air as it enters the head in proximity to the sensitive brain: alternatively, as cooling devices for bodies that were liable to overheat as a consequence of necessarily hectic activity to stay alive in the cold. Either way, the Neanderthal nose makes a plausible adaptation to cold. Their skull shapes, long and low, are by contrast rather more like the skulls of modern people in hot climes – Eskimo skulls are very rounded, evidently again to conserve heat. Strong musculature to balance the big jaws and much-used front teeth of the Neanderthalers may account for their skull shape. Perhaps the Neanderthal folk were endowed with heavy heads of hair to keep in body heat, though there is no reason to think they were hairy all over as some reconstructions depict them. They must have worn clothing of some sort to survive in the winters of their ice age world, though no traces of their clothing have survived, not even as stain marks in some of their graves (as is the case with later ice age burials of early *Homo sapiens sapiens*). Perhaps their dead were never buried in clothes. Clearly, the Neanderthalers generally lacked the bone-working skills to make the sort of toggles and needles their successors went on to use, so their clothes were most likely animal skins made reasonably airtight around their bodies with vegetable strings and rawhide thongs. Their own skin colour may well have been light to maximize the benefit of any sunshine that came their way. Their world might often have resembled the tundra of the frozen north today, but they enjoyed the same

73

seasonal lengths of day as people do now in the same temperate latitudes.

The Neanderthal brain, though large at averages for females of about 1300 ml and for males of 1600 ml, lacked development by comparison with modern *Homo sapiens sapiens* in the neocortical area at the front, where some important higher functions of our brains are thought to be conducted. Certainly, the behaviour of the Neanderthal folk, as evidenced by the archaeological remains they left behind them, did not match the behaviour of their first successors in Europe, who were physically of a type virtually indistinguishable from all of modern humanity and whose archaeological leavings testify to a much greater sophistication all round than was displayed by the Neanderthalers. How much refinement of language use the Neanderthalers may have acquired can only be inferred from their archaeological remains: they left no art products behind them but their Middle Palaeolithic Mousterian tools are an improvement in technique and variety over Lower Palaeolithic artefacts, so it is likely that their speech had advanced somewhat beyond earlier achievements.

(Their vocal tracts were perhaps not as versatile in utterance as ours are, unable to pronounce some of our consonants or distinguish so well between vowels, but the differences certainly do not preclude Neanderthal speech.) What they talked about was still probably of a largely social character, but perhaps starting to handle a wider range of more objective topics like the details of the natural world and the processes of their own technology. There are some signs that their minds were generating more in the way of what we may call ideological content. That they could on occasions support old and diseased members of their groups not able to provide for themselves is evidenced by several cases of chronically sick individuals who survived for some years before death. The Neanderthalers, moreover, sometimes gave deliberate burial to their dead in the floors of caves and rock shelters – dead of both sexes and, frequently, of a very young age. It is difficult to know whether they very often furnished these graves with grave goods like tools or pieces of meat or sprays of flowers (examples of all these things have been claimed), but some of the

Neanderthal burials do seem to have what can only be described as ritual elements like red ochre deposits or, in one case, a covering stone with a carved depression on it. And despite exaggerated claims in the past, there really is some evidence for a bear cult among the Neanderthalers, collecting cave-bear bones and, at a site in France, burying a brown bear's skeleton in a dug grave. Bears were as fond of cave habitation as the Neanderthalers were and rivalry between man and beast must have been a not infrequent event. Bears, moreover, may rear up on their hind legs in a suggestively human way and must have been all round one of the most striking features of the Neanderthalers' world. It would not be so surprising if even the relatively unsophisticated and unimaginative minds of the Neanderthal people were able to conjure up some sort of cult of the bear.

The Neanderthalers no doubt made as much as they could of any plant food available in their often inhospitable world, but trace elements in their teeth confirm what we might expect – that they were predominantly meat eating people. Perhaps they scavenged a good deal of their meat. Scavenging, with its bacterial dangers, is not always a good line to be in but it may be that the often frozen and relatively antiseptic world of the Neanderthalers offered them a niche of opportunity that no other creature could exploit – to drag home and thaw out by their fires the carcasses of deer, horses, reindeer and so forth killed by carnivores or cold and want. At the same time, there is no reason to think the Neanderthalers were not good hunters on occasions. Whether they brought home and shared their meat on the scale that modern foraging people do is open to doubt. Some archaeological evidence has been interpreted to suggest that males may have hogged their catches in their own part of their caves while females and children made do with less meaty food in their separate areas. It is clear, at all events, that life was hard for the Neanderthalers and almost always short – only into the thirties for males, the twenties for females, with high infant mortality and every chance of injury or at least physical stress trauma in the course of their tough, brief lives. (Interestingly, even a case of lung cancer has been identified in a Neanderthal skeleton from a French site.) Neanderthal children matured more quickly than our own, their brains growing rapidly in skulls that were quick to develop the distinctive Neanderthal form. Their childhood time of play and learning was curtailed by comparison with ours.

The study of Neanderthal bones has recently taken a new turn with the extraction of genetic material in at least one case (and it seems there are others under investigation). Fittingly, the first specimen to be examined for surviving traces of DNA is the original 'Neanderthal Man' himself, who was discovered in a quarry in the Neander Dale in Germany in 1856. A sample from an upper arm bone of the 'Neanderthal Man' has yielded a run of mitochondrial DNA (mtDNA) that differs at so many points from the same sequence in modern humans anywhere in the world that biologists have concluded that, at least in respect of their female-descended mtDNA, the Neanderthalers (if they are all like the original 'Neanderthal Man', as is likely) cannot have been directly ancestral to modern humanity. It has been calculated that Neanderthal mtDNA ancestry is likely to have diverged from our own by at least 500,000 BP

– in other words, in the time of *Homo heidelbergensis* if not before. It begins to look to many anthropologists as though *Homo sapiens neanderthalensis* is, as the fossil record already suggests, descended in Europe from *Homo heidelbergensis* but, in the light of mtDNA, not ancestral to European or any other sort of *Homo sapiens sapiens*. Some anthropologists do posit a rather later divergence between the Neanderthal and modern lines, with a last stage of common ancestry represented by fossils found in both Europe and Africa at around 300,000 BP. But few now believe that the Neanderthalers as such can have had much, if any, part in modern human ancestry.

In Africa, there was, as we have seen, a presence of *Homo heidelbergensis* basically like the European situation. Bodo, Elandsfontein and Kabwe are representative of the early stages of African *heidelbergensis* evolution towards *Homo sapiens*. There are some signs that, in Africa, evolution was towards a more modern sort of *Homo sapiens* than took place in Europe with *Homo sapiens neanderthalensis*. No African fossils of early man display the distinctive features of the Neanderthal type, although some of them represent the same general stage of human evolution towards big-brained *sapiens* status. But there are certain fossil finds from Africa that may chart the evolution of our own worldwide subspecies, *Homo sapiens sapiens.* Two skulls from the Omo region in Ethiopia may take the story on from the Kabwe skull of Zambia. Omo II shows a relatively heavily built skull with a noticeably receding forehead but a modern sort of breadth above the ears and a cranial capacity of about 1400 ml. At a date of some 130,000 BP, to go by mollusc shells in the levels in which it was found, Omo II makes a plausible descendant of Kabwe, with progress in brain size and some modernization of skull shape. Omo I, however, is so modern in appearance that some anthropologists fear it may represent an intrusive burial of much later times into the Omo levels: in which case, so might Omo II be. There are other fossils from central and southern Africa that seem to have a similar sort of borderline modern look about them at perhaps the same sort of date as Omo II: from Singa in the Sudan, Ngaloba in Tanzania and Florisbad in South Africa. The fragments of five individuals from

Jebel Ihroud in Morocco show clear signs of human modernity evolving out of something like *Homo heidelbergensis,* at perhaps as early as 150,000 BP. A femur fragment is robust and teeth are large, but a rather delicate jaw shows signs of a chin in the modern manner. (The chin is a jaw-strengthening feature needed after overall reduction of jaw robusticity in modern types.) The Jebel Ihroud skull shape looks primitive at the back but more modern at the front, being broad and flat-faced with hollowed cheeks in marked contrast to the pulled-forward and inflated cheeks of the Neanderthalers who were beginning their career on the north side of the Mediterranean at about the same time. Even so, the Moroccan material shows very rugged brow-ridges by modern standards.

Bones from Border Cave in South Africa have a very modern look to them and might be 100,000 years old, though they were found not by professional archaeologists but by guano shovellers in the 1940s and cannot be securely dated to the levels they seem to come from. Much more reliable and highly persuasive are the bones from Klasies

River Mouth, also in South Africa, professionally excavated in the 1970s. Here the remains of a number of individuals include slender-limbed people without heavy brow-ridges but with some real chin development in most cases (even if teeth were still rather large) dated to between 115,000 and 75,000 BP. From the same site, but from slightly later levels than the human remains, comes some of the earliest evidence in the world for the development of a tool technology to produce narrow blades of stone rather than the broader flakes of Middle Palaeolithic/ Middle Stone Age times. Blades are the hallmark of the Upper Palaeolithic period, associated in Europe with the dazzling culture of the ice age hunters and artists of fully modern physical type. The early blade manifestations of Africa, like some controversial early appearances there of sophisticated bone-working techniques (barbed harpoons found at Katanda in Zaire at a claimed date of about 90,000 BP), did not lead straight on to the Upper Palaeolithic way of life. But it is tempting to relate the pieces of evidence that hint at the evolution of modern humanity in Africa at about 100,000 BP to the archaeological finds of occasional blade-making and bone working in Africa at not so very much later dates. It looks as though the brains of the first more or less fully modern humans were already capable of tentatively trying out new ideas here and there, albeit not very systematically, that would come together tens of thousands of years later as the first flowering of a fully human culture.

FIVE

The Global Species

If we had only the evidence of archaeology to go on, with its (rather meagre) fossil haul from Africa backed up by early African appearances of blade-making and bone working, we might not be so easily persuaded that most of modern humanity's genetic make-up evolved in Africa. But powerful support for that idea has been proposed by geneticists over the last few years.

Mitochondrial DNA has been recovered from the bones of the original 'Neanderthal Man' with the preliminary result, as we have seen, of distancing the Neanderthal people from the line of human descent that leads to ourselves. It may be possible to do similar work on other fossil finds. However, the genetic approach to human evolution is not primarily based on the fossil record from the past but rather on the present state of genetic variation in living human populations, in order to extrapolate back to the likely situation at various stages in the past. It is the nuclear DNA of our cells that controls the development of our inherited characteristics, derived from both parents at conception. The lines of descent of nuclear DNA, as evidenced by the slight variations seen among world populations today, are difficult to trace into the past and it is also difficult to put dates on the appearance of particular variations (on the basis of known rates of genetic mutation). But geneticists have been able to construct family trees of humanity that do suggest an African basis before about 100,000 BP for the genetic make-up of all the peoples of the world, with subsequent separations of populations into distinct variations on the African theme at later dates.

The DNA in the mitochondria of our cells is easier to trace into the past than nuclear DNA for the simple reason that it is transmitted from one generation to the next largely (though perhaps not entirely) from mothers to offspring. (The mitochondria are the power supply units of the cells and have very little to do with inheritance.) The female descent of mtDNA makes it theoretically possible, with the rate of mtDNA mutation calibrated by dated events of primate and human evolution, to track the modern variations of this genetic material back to a source in a single population at a dated time in the past. There are, of course, technical problems with the procedure and complexities arise out of, for example, mutations on top of mutations and the possibility of some paternal inheritance of mtDNA, but for the moment the consensus of research into mtDNA agrees that Africa again appears to be a likely place of origination for the basic mtDNA configuration of all the modern peoples of the world, at some time before 100,000 BP. The various lines of genetic evidence, the fossil finds and the early appearances of technological innovations in Africa, taken together, lend weight to the theory of the African evolution of the best part of the genetic make-up of *Homo sapiens sapiens*. The line from *Homo heidelbergensis* (in the shape of, say, the Bodo skull) through archaic *Homo sapiens* (Kabwe and Jebel Ihroud) to early *Homo sapiens sapiens* (Omo II) is plausibly buttressed by the genetic arguments: an African *sapiens* lineage without the very distinctive traits of the Neanderthalers of Europe and the Levant.

The Levantine situation during the 50,000 years after about 100,000 BP is a very interesting one. There are indications of a proto-Neanderthal presence in the area back into the last interglacial with the skull from Zuttiyeh in Galilee. The small-brained Neanderthal woman from the et-Tabun cave at Mount Carmel may date to an early phase of the last ice age at about 110,000 BP. (She was, perhaps, one of an early Neanderthal band seeking refuge in the milder Levant from the rigours of the ice age in Europe.) But at around 100,000 to 80,000 BP the Mount Carmel caves became the home of the first really unambiguously modern people of early *Homo sapiens sapiens* type that we know. The remains from the caves of es-Skhul and Qafzeh, give or take some ruggedness of brow and prognathism of the jaws (not a bit like the entire mid-face prognathism of the Neanderthalers), really do represent modern physical types, with a rather African physique of long limbs. The interesting thing about them archaeologically is that they were doing next to nothing different from the Neanderthalers in the way of toolmaking or everyday way of life. They made the same Mousterian tools, producing no forward-looking blades or bone work, and they left behind no scrap of art or personal decoration (apart from some traces of ochre). The most that can be said about them is that they do sometimes seem to have placed grave-goods with their dead in a way that is never so clear with the Neanderthal burials of the Levant and Europe, and they seem to have hunted a bit more purposefully than the Neanderthalers. The grave-goods are animal parts (for consumption in a next life?) deliberately placed in contact with the dead, and their hunting prowess is demonstrated by the seasonal selectivity of the animal bones on their sites as opposed to the indiscriminate opportunism of the Neanderthalers all the year round. For the rest, these first representatives of modern humanity, despite their big and well-developed brains, were doing no better than their Neanderthal contemporaries in Europe.

After the early appearances of modern humans in the Levant, the area was again the scene of Neanderthal occupation. Whether the descendants of the moderns retreated into their presumed African homeland or stayed on is hard to say. We have not enough fossils to be sure. Perhaps the moderns and the Neanderthalers were able to coexist in the Levantine area, coming and going without getting in each other's way thanks to their slightly different hunting strategies. Anthropologists who set great store by the genetic evidence theorize that the modern genetic make-up of humanity is all owed to African emigrants who took their genes round the world without interbreeding with local populations of other types they found along the way. But it is worth remembering that, while mtDNA can in theory be traced back to a single source in one population, it is by no means so obvious that some nuclear genetic inheritance among modern peoples cannot have been derived from a variety of sources. There is some indication among the later Neanderthalers of the Levant that a degree of interbreeding with modern types may have taken place.

The export of the modern genetic pattern into the Far East and Australasia may have begun at an early date, not through the Levant but coastally from the Horn of Africa. *Homo sapiens sapiens* seems to have reached Australia by as early as about 60,000 BP (with sea crossings, presumably by raft), and there are signs that some inheritance from the late *Homo erectus* peoples of the Far East may have been incorporated into the stocks that colonized Australia. (The earliest examples of art in Australia may go back to nearly 40,000 BP.)

In the Levantine region, the last of the Neanderthalers faded out after 50,000 BP, and moderns are in evidence in the area by about 40,000 BP. Not only are the bones of the moderns found by this date but also stone tools of the blade-based Upper Palaeolithic type. Sporadic appearances of blades had occurred at various places in North Africa and the Levant at around 70,000 BP only to be followed by a return to Mousterian products; after about 45,000 BP true Upper Palaeolithic tool assemblages were established in these regions, with no reversion to Mousterian. (Along with the tools there are pierced shells for personal ornamentation and other signs of artistic endeavour.) It is reasonable to conclude that both the Mousterian and its Neanderthal makers had made way for *Homo sapiens sapiens* with an Upper Palaeolithic toolmaking tradition. At sites like Boker Tachtit in the Negev and El Wad at Mount Carmel, the local Mousterian appears to have evolved *in situ* into the blade-making Upper Palaeolithic soon after 50,000 BP. When we recall that the early moderns of northern Israel were equipped with Mousterian tool kits back at around 90,000 BP, we may surmise that their successors had finally got around to wholehearted blade-making in a way that the Neanderthalers never did. There seems to be too great a physical difference between even the latest of the Neanderthalers at places like Amud (though they did show just a few traits – like chins on some specimens – that suggest interbreeding with moderns) and the established Upper Palaeolithic people after 40,000 BP to think that the Neanderthalers can have contributed any significant amount of genetic inheritance to the gene pool of the Levantine moderns. No Neanderthal bones are found in this area in association with Upper Palaeolithic tools.

It is possible to track the progress of the blade-based Upper Palaeolithic out of the Levant and into Europe: its spread took place at a time of climatic improvement that would have helped its makers to go north into a Europe that had previously been too cold for them. At Ksar Akil in Lebanon, a proper Upper Palaeolithic industry dates to about 44,000 BP, while the oldest Upper Palaeolithic of Europe that has been discovered so far dates to before 43,000 BP in the form of the Aurignacian material from Bacho Kiro in Bulgaria. The Aurignacian is the earliest of the succession of Upper Palaeolithic cultures in Europe, widespread from east to west. Whereas there are transitional industries in the Negev and Israel to demonstrate the evolution of the Upper Palaeolithic out of the Mousterian, no such Mousterian on its way to Aurignacian has been discovered anywhere in Europe. The Aurignacian, moreover, arrives as a remarkably uniform cultural expression across from Eastern to Western Europe, more uniform in fact than the range of local

Mousterian variants that precede it. In Europe, the Mousterian has never been found with anything but Neanderthal bones: nor the Aurignacian with anything other than those of *Homo sapiens sapiens.*

The Aurignacian is a very distinctive toolmaking tradition, with an emphasis on narrow blades from carefully prepared cores (rather than the broad flakes of the Mousterian) and bone and ivory points that are signally missing from Mousterian assemblages. From the first, it displays those elements of personal adornment and artistic production already seen in the Levantine Upper Palaeolithic. It seems to have spread across Europe from east to west in a matter of a few thousands of years, its progress charted at sites in Croatia and Moravia at well over 35,000 years ago, in Germany not much later, reaching south-west France and Spain by at least 34,000 BP (and probably rather earlier according to the latest revisions of radiocarbon dating). The best known find of the bones of early moderns to go with the spread of the Aurignacian was made in the Crô-Magnon rock shelter in the French Dordogne – the site has given its name to the entire race of early *Homo sapiens sapiens* in Europe. There are a few places (in southern Russia, Hungary and Italy) where late Mousterian levels appear to show a cultural episode with a mixture of Mousterian and Aurignacian traits that may be the results either of natural or archaeological confusion of the materials or, just possibly, of short-lived instances of acculturation when Neanderthalers somehow took on board some of the innovations of the Aurignacian people. A case has been made for the survival of a few Neanderthal physical traits (seen in details of skull shapes, teeth and jaws) among some of the early *Homo sapiens sapiens* people found in association with Aurignacian material in Central and Eastern Europe: it seems as though a certain amount of interbreeding may have gone on here, with the input of a small amount of Neanderthal inheritance into the early modern populations. (In Portugal, a four-year-old child's bones, dated to about 24,500 BP, have been deemed to show, alongside perfectly modern teeth and chin formation, some surviving Neanderthal traits of stockiness of trunk and leg bones.) Again, the short time interval separating the last of the Neanderthalers and their Mousterian tools from the first of the moderns and their Aurignacian implements appears to rule out any large-scale evolution from Neanderthal to modern types in Europe, even if there was a certain amount of interbreeding. Some anthropologists deny that the apparently Neanderthal-like features of some of the early moderns (and they are very slight) are owed to anything more than coincidence.

In south-west France and northern Spain, archaeologists have found evidence of a brief cultural event that really does look like a clear case of Neanderthal acculturation under the influence of the incoming Upper Palaeolithic. For a few thousand years an industrial tradition, called Chatelperronian, after one of its find sites, flourished with a basically late Mousterian assemblage of tool types (side-scrapers, notched flakes, blunt-backed knives, etc.) to which were added such Upper Palaeolithic elements as true blades, end-scrapers, sharp-ended burins, some bone and antler tools and items of adornment like perforated animal teeth. At one Chatelperronian site a rough circle of eleven post holes enclosed a

4 m-wide area partially paved with limestone slabs and incorporating two hearths: the holes were probably for mammoth bones (abundant on the site) as structural elements of a hut. Hut building with this sophistication and personal decoration are behavioural traits never attested in any earlier Mousterian contexts. At three sites the Chatelperronian is interleaved with Aurignacian levels, a situation indicating the contemporaneity of the two traditions at a date around 34,000 BP. At the site of Saint-Césaire, a fairly complete human skeleton was found in association with Chatelperronian material: it was the skeleton of a classic Neanderthal type, with no signs of any interbreeding with moderns or evolution from Neanderthal to modern type. The likeliest explanation of the Chatelperronian phenomenon remains that it was developed by late Neanderthalers of previously Mousterian habits in response to the arrival in their midst of moderns with the Upper Palaeolithic Aurignacian culture. It would appear that the two rather different peoples were able to coexist for quite a while, evidently with some contact but perhaps no great conflict, for the Aurignacian

hunters were again more sophisticated in their hunting strategies and had more specialized targets. But the Chatelperronian was a geographically limited affair that did not outlive the end of the Mousterian in general. By about 30,000 BP the last had been seen of the Neanderthalers in France and Spain and, with them, all traces of Mousterian manufacture of any kind. We need not picture any extermination of the Neanderthalers by the Crô-Magnons: just a bit better success at the hunt, a bit higher birth rate and lower level of infant mortality could have given the moderns the advantage to outcompete the Neanderthalers over the space of a few thousand years. But the fact that some Neanderthalers were able to acculturate at all to elements of the Aurignacian way of life is striking: in particular, the adoption of personal ornamentation impresses, since this practice is associated with a developed sense of self *vis-à-vis* others in complex social relations, expressed in a symbolic way. The Neanderthalers might never have hit upon it by themselves, but evidently they were able to respond to the idea at some level.

We saw that the first of the moderns, back in Israel at 90,000 or more years ago, were scarcely living any differently from their Neanderthal contemporaries, making the same tools, producing no items of personal decoration or works of art, only perhaps hunting a little better and sometimes burying their dead with indisputable grave-goods. By contrast, the Aurignacians of some 50,000 or so years later – though not obviously any more evolved physically – were wielding a tool kit vastly superior to the Mousterian, building bigger and better shelters with proper hearths for their fires, wearing adornments of pierced bone and shells and producing works of art unparalleled at any previous stage of human evolution. Some anthropologists have speculated about an invisible modification of brain performance that may have arisen by mutation (and then been fostered by natural selection for its usefulness) between the time of the Skhul and Qafzeh moderns and the Crô-Magnon people. But it is equally possible that the moderns were, from the first, equipped with brains of great potential that only showed itself initially in slightly better hunting strategies, with grave-goods, and a more vivid response to death. It needed the elaboration of culture as a force in its own right to get the best out of the moderns' minds. The technological innovations of blade-making and bone work that had previously only made intermittent marks became firmly established after 50,000 BP. Language use probably saw a similar process of sophistication, with more grammatical detail and precision. Above all, it seems likely that the previously com- partmentalized minds of our remoter ancestors became integrated for the first time. Mental domains that had before dealt separately (and largely unconsciously) with technology, with natural history lore, with hunting practices, with sexual activity, with provision for offspring and so forth were brought together into the superdomain of social consciousness and, henceforth, subjected to the same sort of introspection and creative imagination that had hitherto been reserved for the business of social interactions. Not surprisingly, newly integrated minds with a long history of socially orientated consciousness were prone from the first (as ours still are) to anthropomorphize enthusiastically (and fruitfully, as well as dangerously) about the whole wide world. It comes naturally to us to think that everything works like ourselves: we credit the external world with the instincts, desires, intentions, purposes, reactions of which we are conscious in ourselves. In pre-scientific times, our ancestors imputed spirits to the animal world (even to trees): in scientific thought, too, the notion of entities or 'forces' behind natural phenomena (like gravity, for example) is hard to shake off.

To judge by the art of the Upper Palaeolithic people, the animal world was of great significance in their consciousness, and not just for its food value. There may well have been an element of hunting magic in the cave art, but it evidently had a profound social dimension that bound people together in what we might as well call a religious spirit. From well before 30,000 BP come the animal paintings of the Chauvet cave in France: some of them are naturalistic pictures of horses, rhino, lions, but there is at least one case of a composite figure mixing human and animal features – human for the bottom half and bison for the top. From the Höhlenstein-Stadel cave in southern Germany comes a carved ivory figure also from well before 30,000 BP that combines a human body with a lion's head. The anthropomorphizing tendency is very clear in artistic productions like these: the human imagination can here be seen to have got to work on the world in a way never glimpsed before. There was a positive cult, widespread across Europe, of small human female statuary in stone, bone, ivory, even baked clay after a while, at whose potential meanings we can only guess. And there are various representations of the human sex organs carved in stone, particularly vulvae: with the inauguration of the integrated mind of the moderns, the sexual – previously conducted, like so much else, on automatic pilot, as it were – would have become the imaginatively erotic, with enormous impact on all aspects of human behaviour.

A new sort of mind in action is similarly evidenced by the burials of the Upper Palaeolithic people: there are beads and ornaments in the graves, some evidence of tailored clothes with decorative fringes of beads, indications of different dress codes for the sexes, real cemeteries with multiple interments. In one case a crippled young woman was buried arms linked with one male and next to another whose right arm reached over to her pubic region, where red ochre was splashed around. Make of such a scene what we will, there was nothing like it in the Middle Palaeolithic!

There are noticeably more Upper Palaeolithic sites than Middle Palaeolithic ones and raw materials – like favoured qualities of flint or precious stones for personal ornament – were transported over much greater distances. There was plainly a wider network of contacts between bigger populations. There was also much more cultural diversification, geographically and over time, once the initially uniform Aurignacian tradition began to evolve. The climatic amelioration that ushered the moderns and the Aurignacian into Europe did not last: a steady deterioration led on by about 18,000 BP to the very severest of ice age conditions, worse than anything the Neanderthalers had faced. The Upper Palaeolithic people rose to the challenge and began, indeed, to occupy areas in Siberia where humanity had never ventured before.

The Neanderthalers had never built the large, heated structures of the East European early moderns.

The Gravettian tradition, which replaced the Aurignacian after about 28,000 BP, saw a great elaboration in open-site living on the plains of Eastern Europe where there were no caves to inhabit. In Russia (where the salmon runs of rivers like the Don provided a newly exploited basis of subsistence) there were sites with elaborate houses built of scores of mammoth bones that show a progression from communal arrangements with shared storage pits to the concentration of stores in huts bigger than all the rest, as though chiefs and/or medicine men were rising to control in a much more complex and hierarchically organized form of human society than had ever been seen before. Gravettian toolmaking put its emphasis on small and parallel-sided blades often pointed and very steeply retouched along one edge (to create blunt backs), with bone awls and punches but no Aurignacian bone points. For a few thousand years around 20,000 BP the very distinctive Solutrean culture flourished in France, producing a range of bifacial, leaf-shaped flints of exceptional workmanship. In Siberia, a Gravettian sort of tradition with bifacially worked spear points is the background to the culture that early man carried into the Americas, perhaps from about 20,000 BP onwards and certainly, in force, after about 13,000 BP – over millennia when the extreme cold of the last ice age had lowered sea levels to permit a crossing over the Bering Strait into Alaska.

In Europe, the Magdalenian tradition began at about 18,000 BP, to pass thereafter through many phases, with great abundance and variety of bone and antler work, some of it highly decorative, and a range of often tiny flint products that were clearly employed in composite tools with bone and wooden handles. (Microlithic stone work, and the beginnings of art, too, go back to beyond 20,000 BP in Africa.) Bone needles were pioneered in Eastern Europe by about 22,000 BP (a few thousand years later in the west); the spear-thrower was joined by the bow and arrow by about 13,000 BP. Some of the finest and most famous of the cave art belongs to the Magdalenian period which, with its immediate derivatives, persisted right to the end of the last ice age in Western Europe.

Baking of shaped clay to make figurines was first developed in Central Europe at about 28,000 BP, but no fired pottery containers were made anywhere until as late as about 9,000 BP (in Mesopotamia and the Far East – with claims for some pots in Japan at a slightly earlier date). Pottery is one of the key features of the Neolithic, the time of the first farmers after the end of the last ice age, though there was farming before there was pot-making. Crop growing does not extend back into the ice age but, in a part of the world well away from the northern glaciers, it is possible to detect the first inklings of the use of cereals as a major component of diet. From Egypt at a date of around 17–15,000 BP (when the last ice age was at its fiercest in Europe and the civilization of the ancient Egyptians was still some 12,000 years away) come grindstones and flint sickle blades strongly suggesting the harvesting of wild grasses and preparation of cereal grains. The sickle blades sometimes carry a gloss produced by the cutting of grass stems. It would be another 8,000 years or so before deliberate cultivation of crops was undertaken, together with

105

the domestication of animals, but it is clear that late glacial times saw the foundation work for all that was to come in the postglacial world of the first farmers and then the first civilizations. Technological progress in toolmaking, the first tentative steps towards the farming mode of subsistence, the emergence of social hierarchy, the obvious importance of the artistic impulse, the clear operation of ideological motives to do with hunting and death and sex – all these things indicate how far physical and cultural evolution had carried humanity, not just from our ape ancestry of 6 mya but also from our immediate predecessors like the Neanderthalers of Europe and even the early moderns of the Levant.

Once the physical structure of the brain that works the integrated mind of the moderns was in place, it was to be cultural rather than further physical evolution that would take on the story of humanity. Culture has been likened to a second system of inheritance to go alongside nuclear DNA – only it works much faster and an individual does not need to be genetically related to another in order to inherit ideas and patterns of behaviour. The wide distribution of the small female statuary of Aurignacian and Gravettian times (the so-called 'venuses') shows that culture was embracing geographically separated people, not closely related by birth, in a web of ideas and beliefs. It is fascinating to speculate about the languages of those times: we can be certain that the modern sort of language use, with high symbolic content, was well established among these sophisticated people. The universal language of music seems also to have been one of their accomplishments: there are holed bone tubes that can be played today as flutes, and depictions in their art of people apparently playing wind and even string instruments; a mammoth skull was found with a well-dented brow that may have been played as a drum.

In northern Europe, the ice age ended with a series of oscillations of warm and cold over a period of about 2,500 years, with the world restored to at least the warmth of today by 10,000 years ago (and sea levels beginning to rise again, too). The late Magdalenian hunters of northern France and Germany specialized in the hunting of reindeer with the bow and arrow to the point where we can almost suspect that herding was being developed. But the ice age world was soon to disappear, with the reindeer driven north after their own food supplies, to be replaced in the spreading woodlands by red, fallow and roe deer. Open-country animals like the horse largely disappeared too – in Siberia, there is every likelihood that the mammoth was finally hunted to extinction. As the Upper Palaeolithic way of life gave way to the Mesolithic, the high culture of the Magdalenian hunter-artists fell away into a bit of uninspired sketching on bones and colouring of pebbles. But there was technological innovation in Mesolithic Europe, with yet more emphasis on microlithic flints for composite tools together with bone harpoons for fishing and a new pattern of axes for woodworking.

The epicentre of spectacular progress in human affairs moved away from Europe in postglacial times. It was to be once more in the area of the Levant and its wider context in the Fertile Crescent, stretching from the Zagros mountains in the east to the Nile valley in the west, that the beginnings of plant cultivation and animal domestication would be made. (Similar beginnings would be made, too, in other parts of the world, sometimes quite independently.) In the wake of farming and settled living with surpluses of food would come civilization with hierarchy, bureaucracy, writing, even the first invention of the wheel! Humanity at various earlier stages of evolution had emerged into warmer, wetter postglacial worlds on half a dozen previous occasions, as the great ice ages of the past had melted into interglacial times – but on no former occasion had humanity gone on to such a panoply of innovation as happened after the close of our latest ice age. On no former occasion had there been any modern-minded *Homo sapiens sapiens* around to do it.

Glossary

Acheulian   The widespread early toolmaking tradition with stone axes.

anthropomorphism   The human tendency to impute human characteristics to non-human things and processes.

Aurignacian   The first of the **Upper Palaeolithic** cultures of the Levant and Europe.

Australopithecines   The range of specialized apes that stand at the start of the hominid line leading, with hindsight, to humanity.

bifacial   A stone tool worked on both sides rather than left with one face unmodified.

bipedalism   Walking upright on two legs.

blade   A struck **flake** of stone at least twice as long as it is wide.

BP   Before the present.

core   The primary piece of stone from which **flakes** were struck, either to render the core into a tool or produce flake tools or both.

cranial capacity   The internal brain space in the skull, averaging about 1200 ml in women and 1500 ml in men today.

110

DNA Dioxyribonucleic acid, the molecules of which carry the genetic information to organize living cells and control the inheritance of characterisitcs.

flake A piece struck off a **core** of stone to shape the core into a tool or to function as a tool in its own right (not twice as long as it is wide – see **blade**).

gracile Of slender as opposed to robust build of body or skull.

grave-goods Items such as tools or ornaments or food offerings deliberately placed in association with buried bodies.

hand-axe The distinctive **core**-based tool of the Acheulian tradition.

hominids The family of specialized apes and ex-apes, including the Australopithecines at one end and ourselves at the other, that comprises the evolution of humanity.

Hominoidea The zoological superfamily to which all the forms of ape and humanity belong.

Homo The genus (group of closely related species) that includes all the toolmaking human types of the past two million years.

knuckle-walking The distinctive mode of locomotion of the gorillas and chimps, going on all fours with their long arms supported on the backs of their bent fingers.

Lower Palaeolithic The earlier part of the Old Stone Age, with hand-axes or simple flake tools, called Early Stone Age in Africa.

Middle Palaeolithic The stage of Old Stone Age toolmaking characterized by less emphasis on axes and more sophistication of flake tool manufacture (called Middle Stone Age in Africa).

Mousterian The particular form of the Middle Palaeolithic seen in Europe and the Levant, often associated with the Neanderthal people.

mitochondrial DNA The **DNA** in the mitochondria (energy supply units) on living cells, playing little or no part in generational inheritance of characteristics and descending mostly, if not entirely, from mother to offspring.

mya Millions of years ago.

natural selection The mechanism whereby random mutations from one generation to the next are selected by blind nature for their capacity to enhance (or degrade) survival chances, and are thus preserved or deleted in the course of evolution.

ochre Natural pigments, usually red, garnered by our ancestors, presumably to colour something in their lives, or themselves.

Oldowan The toolmaking tradition, with crude **core** and **flake** tools, that preceded the Acheulian.

pongids The ape family that includes the chimps, gorillas and orang-utans, but not the gibbons.

postcranial The skeleton below the skull.

primates The mammalian order to which all human beings past and present belong, together with apes, monkeys, lemurs, tarsiers and even less obviously related creatures like the tree shrews.

prognathism   Forward projection of the jaw area of the face.

retouch   Secondary work on a struck **flake** of stone to improve its use as a tool.

sexual dimorphism   The situation of extreme physical difference (in size and ruggedness, for example) between males and females.

Tayacian   The sort of late Lower Palaeolithic toolmaking on **flakes** that gave rise to the **Mousterian** tradition.

Upper Palaeolithic   The later era of the Old Stone Age, with sophisticated manufacture of **blade** tools and weapons and implements of bone, called Late Stone Age in Africa.

Further Reading

Among the books listed with full publication details below the most up-to-date detailed account of human evolution is contained in Roger Lewin's *Human Evolution, An Illustrated Introduction*; Glenn C. Conroy's *Reconstructing Human Origins* is a clear and attractive work; for quite wonderful photographs of the fossil finds and a valuable text, Johanson's *From Lucy to Language* must be seen. James Shreeve's *The Neandertal Enigma* covers in a colourful style the controversial matter of the eclipse of the Neanderthalers and the emergence of modern humanity. Steven Mithen's *The Prehistory of the Mind* is an essential introduction to the key topic of mental evolution. *The Neanderthals, Changing the Image of Mankind* by Trinkhaus and Shipman is a thorough and rewarding account of the whole history of the discovery of our fossil ancestors and of the sometimes controversial personalities and interpretations that go with the finds.

114

FURTHER READING

Cavalli-Sforza, Luca and Francesco, *The Great Human Diasporas*, Reading, Massachusetts, Addison Wesley, 1995

Conroy, Glenn C., *Reconstructing Human Origins*, New York and London, W.W. Norton & Co., 1997

Deacon, Terence, *The Symbolic Species*, London, Allen Lane, 1997

Dennett, Daniel, *Consciousness Explained*, London, Penguin Books, 1993

Foley, Robert, *Humans before Humanity*, Oxford, Blackwell, 1997

Gamble, Clive, *Timewalkers : The Prehistory of Global Colonization*, Cambridge Massachusetts, Harvard University Press, 1994

Gowlett, John A.J., *Ascent to Civilization*, New York and London, McGraw-Hill, 1993

Johanson, Donald and Edgar, Blake, *From Lucy to Language*, New York, Simon & Schuster, 1996

Jones, S., Martin, R., and Pilbeam, D., (eds), *Cambridge Encylopaedia of Human Evolution*, Cambridge University Press, 1992

Klein, Richard G., *The Human Career*, Chicago University Press, 1989

Lewin, Roger, *Principles of Human Evolution*, Oxford, Blackwell, 1998

——, *Human Evolution, An Illustrated Introduction*, Oxford, Blackwell, 1999

Mithen, Steven, *The Prehistory of the Mind*, London, Thames & Hudson, 1996

Pinker, Steven, *How the Mind Works*, New York, W.W. Norton, 1997, and London, Allen Lane, The Penguin Press, 1998

Shreeve, James, *The Neandertal Enigma, Solving the Mystery of Modern Human Origins*, London, Penguin Books, 1997

Stringer, Christopher and Gamble, Clive, *In Search of the Neanderthals*, London, Thames & Hudson, 1993

Stringer, Christopher and McKie, Robin, *African Exodus*, London, Jonathan Cape, 1996

Tattersall, Ian, *The Fossil Trail*, Oxford University Press, 1995

Trinkaus, Erik and Shipman, Pat, *The Neanderthals, Changing the Image of Mankind*, London, Jonathan Cape, 1993

Walker, Alan and Shipman, Pat, *The Wisdom of Bones*, New York, Alfred A. Knopf, 1996 and London, Weidenfeld & Nicolson, 1996

Index

Bold type indicates main or more significant entries